CONTENTS

D0110000

3

THE NEW MOOD IN LUTHERAN WORSHIP

Herbert F. Lindemann

AUGSBURG PUBLISHING HOUSE
MINNEAPOLIS, MINNESOTA

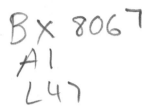

THE NEW MOOD IN LUTHERAN WORSHIP

Manufactured in the United States of America

FOREWORD

There is a new mood in Lutheran worship. It is the result of a new phase of the so-called liturgical movement. Until publication in 1958 of the *Service Book and Hymnal,* mainstream liturgical development among Lutherans in North America had as its primary goal the recovery of a lost heritage. A cogent rite exhibiting the best of our heritage could be instrumental in achieving liturgical uniformity among our congregations.

The crucial steps had been taken when the *Common Service* became normative in books used by most Lutherans, e.g. the *Common Service Book,* the *American Lutheran Hymnal,* the *Lutheran Hymnal.* The *Service Book and Hymnal* is both the achievement of and the monument to many who had to struggle for vital and intelligent worship, often against ridicule and censure.

5

But the beginnings of the new mood are there also where the *SBH* goes beyond Lutheran consensus to greater ecumenical awareness.

Since 1958 the ecumenical dimension of liturgical renewal has increased, coupled with a growing awareness of the interrelation of worship and mission. Worship must be seen in terms of the whole Christian life, and vice versa. Liturgical concerns cannot be separated from ethical concerns. One observes the new mood in the veritable eruption of experimental services as well as in openness to popular styles of music. Varied though they are, these services tend to be intensely corporate and possess an infectious spirit of celebration. Since 1966 the Inter-Lutheran Commission on Worship (the first truly pan-Lutheran liturgical group) has been Lutheranism's official exponent of the new direction in liturgical renewal. Experimentation needs to go forward both on the parish and denominational levels. The two types need each other so that local creativity is balanced by the needs of the broader church.

Pastor Lindemann is extraordinarily qualified to write about the change in direction. His professional life has been invested in the liturgical movement. Through several key posts he has furthered a venturing spirit, refusing to be content with past achievements, solid though they have been. But, in unfolding the story, he omits his own significant role. He is chairman of the Valparaiso

Institute for Liturgical Studies; his previous publications have enriched our life of worship; he was prominent in drafting the *Worship Supplement* (LC—MS); he was among the catalyst group which brought the Inter-Lutheran Commission on Worship into being, and served as its first chairman; as chairman he convened the ecumenical Consultation on Common Texts; he is a member of the international *Societas Liturgica*.

But perhaps his most significant work has been done in the parishes he has served. He has not been content to theorize; his pastoral ministry is proof of the validity of his concept of the church.

This is, in many ways, a personal book. It makes claims neither to completeness nor to detached analysis. The author writes out of his experience as a clergyman in the Lutheran Church —Missouri Synod, and he writes as a pastor. The scholarly work on the transitional phase of liturgical renewal among Lutherans still remains to be written. But when it is, its author will be indebted to what is contained between these covers. Here it is available first hand from one who is directly involved.

EUGENE BRAND
Director of Commission on Worship
Lutheran Church in America
New York

1

LITURGICAL CHAOS:
BEGINNINGS OF A MOVEMENT

The problems of contemporary society are so huge, so threatening, so much discussed that everything else seems to be of decidedly minor importance. Every day, on every possible platform the debate continues concerning race relations, war, the pollution of air and water, the decay of our cities, dope addiction, sexual excesses and perversions, the revolt of the young, unrest on college campuses, and similar problems. These issues fill our minds; they press so strongly for solutions that we are inclined to shelve all other matters, at least temporarily. We seem to be fighting for nothing less than survival, and when the situation is that desperate, men have no time or energy to deal with lesser concerns.

One of the interest areas which has been shunted onto a sidetrack is liturgics. Thirty-five

9

years ago, in the Lutheran church of this country, interest in liturgics was at a peak. The Liturgical Society of St. James was organized in 1927 and held its first mid-western conference in Detroit in 1933. The emotional explosion touched off by this meeting was indeed something to behold. Men smelled "Romanism" a mile away from the church where the conference was held. Clergymen and laymen alike were astounded that anyone should seriously advocate the introduction of eucharistic vestments, Gregorian chant, weekly communions, the sign of the cross, kneeling for prayer, and—horror of horrors—even incense! Such practices vitiated the pure gospel; they would certainly emphasize form and ceremony at the expense of doctrine. Preaching would deteriorate; worship would become mere routine. People would think of obedience to the rubrics as somehow meritorious, and if they were well versed in what to do and when to do it they would consider themselves to be a cut above those who were not possessed of this esoteric knowledge. Furthermore, if they received Holy Communion too often, it would become commonplace, and they would tend to commune without adequate preparation. The sacrament should remain precious, but as a bonus in the Christian life, a devotional luxury. The main thing has to be the preaching of the gospel.

So the argument ran, and it must be admitted

that some of the more enthusiastic promoters of the liturgical movement of the 1930s did invite such criticisms and warnings. Reformers and crusaders are always too intense; they have to be to get their point across. But their opponents, past and present, would do well to consider the causes of the movement so abhorrent to them. There was justification for the Liturgical Society of St. James, a justification which was quite evident in church life a half-century ago. Lutheranism of that time was in the doldrums. The pre-war theological giants, the pioneers and the protagonists of the doctrinal controversies were dead and gone; high-calibre successors were scarce. Much of the church retained a definitely European cast, although some of this was rather forcibly shed during the First World War. The period between the two wars was a low point in theological thought and devotional life. Lutheranism was in the process of becoming americanized. It had not yet completely cut its cultural ties with Europe—neither had it come into its own in the new world. Another world war would accelerate the process, and the post-war rush of events would sweep the church into the mainstream of American life; but that time was not yet. In the 1920s and 30s the church seemed to be immovably anchored on dead center. It was still living in the past. It had not embraced the future, and the present was

11

utterly bewildering. It was a church which had not found itself.

The proponents of the liturgical movement turned their spotlight on the church's devotional and sacramental life and so exposed certain facts which were not at all palatable to more institutionally minded churchmen. Much the same situation prevails in officialdom today—ecclesiastical officials, with very few exceptions, have been markedly apathetic to the concerns of their liturgically minded brethren.

Liturgical Chaos

The following characteristics may be noted of the church 40 to 50 years ago: The country abounded in architectural monstrosities. The older Lutheran church buildings were better than the newer ones, but they tended to have the same pattern: shallow chancels, high pulpits, a statue of Thorvaldsen's Christ above the altar, the altar itself white enameled, electric candelabra, no seasonal colors in the paraments. The newer churches were abominations to God and man. Architects had no idea of the genius of Lutheran worship, and parochial building committees even less. The result was that Lutherans put up nondescript buildings: four walls and a roof, and not much else, except some horrible green glass windows.

After a few decades of this a reaction was sure to set in, and it did: there was a Gothic revival. Its leaders were Ralph Adams Cram and Charles Goodhue, and between them they succeeded in erecting some truly beautiful churches: Trinity Church in Detroit and Trinity Church in Fort Wayne are two Lutheran examples which readily come to mind. F. R. Webber for many years was the leading Lutheran exponent of the Gothic revival, presenting his views in the *American Lutheran* and voluminous correspondence. The trouble with this type of architecture, however, was its enormous expense. Most congregations could not afford the genuine article, and as a result, ersatz Gothic churches went up all over the country, with sometimes ghastly results. The time was ripe for the evolution of a modern style; but in the 30s that time had not yet come.

With the poor architecture there was a great deal of gingerbread art. The use of symbolism was very limited and often ill-advised. First-rate paintings were not to be seen anywhere. Statuary was stereotype. Banners were not thought of. Liturgical colors were not in general use, with the result that church interiors tended to look drab and uninteresting, always the same, year after year. As for music, it was atrocious. The only bright spots in the musical spectrum were the chorale tunes enshrined in the hymnals, but these were so often played and sung at funeral tempos that the faithful were alienated from their own heritage. Edward Rechlin went around the country playing organ recitals, trying to awaken interest in and appreciation for the music of Johann Sebastian Bach, but there was little he could do on a continuing basis beyond training church musicians for work in their own congregations.

In some churches it was common practice to ask parochial school teachers to function as organists and choirmasters on the side—which imposed an almost impossible burden on them and ruled out any first-rate program of music. It was difficult to say which suffered most in those days: organ or choir. What should the choir sing? Only one set of arrangements for the introits and graduals had been published: by H. Alexander Matthews, in 1924. Anthems were in the Moody-Sankey idiom; a prominent music publisher of that day was the Lorenz Company, which was not distinguished for favoring classical chorale tunes. But little else was available, and most choirmasters were no better trained than to ape the work of their Protestant neighbors down the street. The period was not destined to go down in history for its musical excellence.

The music of the liturgy was unvarying. Antecommunion was the almost universal order for Sunday morning, except for those more or less infrequent occasions on which the sacrament was celebrated. Matins, though printed out in some hymnals, was unknown and unused. Vespers was still sung in some churches, but the setting of the Magnificat left much to be desired. The Psalms, the Venite, the Te Deum, the Benedictus and other canticles were never heard; alternate lessons to the standard Epistles and Gospels were seldom read—all of which reduced the diet of Holy Scripture to a bare subsistence minimum. And the liturgical music, as has already been implied, was insufferably monotonous. Some of it was not very good to begin with, notably the chant for the Gloria in Excelsis. Seen as a whole, the music for the Eucharist was a hodge-podge; some of it had a Gregorian flavor, some came from the German *Kirchenordnungen,* and the much-martyred setting for the Gloria was (and still is in some services!) a "Scottish Chant." This musical amalgam was ground together every Sunday morning, year after year, decade after decade. No one even thought of an alternate setting.

The result was a horrible sterility. Doing the liturgy was not something to be enjoyed; it was a routine which the church, for mysterious reasons of its own, imposed upon her children. The idea was to get through it as painlessly as possible and so to arrive at the chief business of the morning: the sermon. This imposed an additional burden on the preacher; not only was his utterance to be spell-binding in its own right, but he somehow had to counterbalance the deadening effects of the liturgical "preliminaries" just concluded. It was enough to tax the prowess of the ablest pulpiteer.

Few, if any, understood what the liturgy was all about. That's not to be wondered at, because almost no one took the trouble to explain it to the people. And the reason for that was that the pastors themselves did not understand it and had no appreciation for its genuis. In their minds too, the sermon was "the thing," and the rest of the service was merely the setting for the homiletic jewel.

In such a pervasive silence concerning things liturgical, it was only natural that there should be some misunderstanding and a certain amount of faulty practice. Thus, it was common to think of the Kyrie as an act of penitence rather than as a litany response, as it is used in the *Service Book and Hymnal* and the Worship Supplement. The Offertory was treated as an appendage to the sermon, giving the congregation a welcome seventh-inning stretch after sitting through the preacher's lengthy utterance. There was, of course, no eucharistic prayer; it was not even dreamed of. On the other hand, there were numerous subtractions from the printed order of service, and a great many transpositions of the various elements.

Theodore Graebner wrote an essay describing the practices of this period and called it, "Our Liturgical Chaos." It was both amusing and sad.

The liturgical "howlers" chronicled in this essay were so atrocious as to be really funny, but at the same time it was sobering to consider that clergymen, whose main business in life was to lead people into a deeper and richer communion with God, should be guilty of such things. They were not to be blamed too much, however, for their training in the art of worship was minimal. At most Lutheran seminaries at that time, there was but one course in liturgics. It was usually given for one semester only, and for two or three hours a week. (Unhappily this situation is not greatly improved, even today.)

The most depressing characteristic of eucharistic worship in the 20s and 30s was the spirit in which it was conducted. First of all, it was customary in these days to precede the communion with a confessional service 15 to 30 minutes long. This had its value, but it also had two disadvantages: it prolonged the time communicants were expected to be in church, thus creating the impression that receiving the sacrament was something of a bore; and it intensified a widespread feeling that going to communion was a very sombre experience, in which people were to dwell on their sinfulness, being fearful of receiving the sacrament "unworthily," to their own damnation. There was little joy in the whole experience. The melancholy mood of it was often expressed in the manner in which the liturgy was played and sung:

slowly, ponderously, as though the congregation were assembled for a funeral rather than the wedding feast of the Lamb. Small wonder that people dragged their feet in coming to the sacrament! In 1930 Lutherans received Holy Communion an average of about twice per year.

Having become somewhat critical of the pastors of that era, let us take the criticism a step further. They paid little or no attention to corporate worship; they concentrated on preaching. But what was the preaching like? It was like the liturgy in one way: it was boring. The sermons were poured into an unvarying mold: introduction, theme and parts, conclusion. That's sensible enough, although one often wished that occasionally a preacher might stand everything on its ear, just to be different.

The uniform structure might have been endured if there had been some variety in the material. There wasn't much. Most sermons dealt with the doctrine of justification by faith, or some facet thereof. Little was heard about sanctification; preachers seemed afraid of giving the impression that a man could be saved by good works, apart from faith. Faith, however, seemed largely a matter of subscribing to the church's doctrine. Not much was said about one's personal relationship to God as this was implemented in the situations of daily life. Life-situation preaching, as it later came to be known, was quite rare, at least in most

18

Lutheran pulpits. The sermons were definitely theological, and most people—let's face it—are not much interested in theology, unless they can see some connection between it and their life in between Sundays. This was often the missing link in the sermons of that era. They were irrelevant.

What a great thing it is to discover a church in which there is good preaching and a rich worship life! In many churches of the 20s and 30s there was neither, and the writer of these lines searched diligently during his college days, during his years at the seminary, and in his year of internship. The results were disappointing; there was only one church in Fort Wayne and one in St. Louis which met the double test. In a few other parishes there was a flicker of life in one way or another, but generally one got the impression either that the pastor himself was too hidebound to let the Holy Spirit take over, or the congregation was so comfortable in its somnolence that it did not permit the pastor to do what he knew he ought to do.

In any event, the church was dull and dead. If today we are disturbed by the alienation of young people from established religion, we can look back to the churches of a half-century ago and wish that these had had a far greater awareness of the rut into which they had fallen and a far greater surrender to the God who was summoning them to meet the challenge of a new era. Now that this new day has come, the church has great difficulty in making up lost time, in effecting the adjustments which should have been initiated decades ago.

Beginnings of a Movement

It is useless to cry over lost opportunities. The only purpose of the foregoing has been to indicate the cause and justification for the liturgical movement. For, while a widespread impression prevailed that this movement was concerned with all sorts of peripheral niceties—the cut of a surplice, the length of a stole, positioning at the altar, how to make the sign of the cross, when to stand, sit, and kneel—its chief concern actually was the renewal of the church's life. Perhaps some of the pioneers did not realize the implications, but this basically was what the movement was about.

At the same time other things were happening in the church—much more quietly, but nonetheless very significantly. Biblical scholars were speaking out with a new honesty and this had, and continues to have explosive repercussions. Luther scholarship was being renewed, resulting, among other things, in a new translation and a definitive English edition of Luther's works. Social workers were sharpening their philosophies and improving their techniques, and the beginnings of a Christian stance toward race relations were to be detected. All these stirrings were indications of an incipient revival and renewal of the life of the church. It was high time. The period of the 20s and 30s was a nadir.

Liturgical changes were the most obvious symptoms of the new spirit; and they affected all church members—not only those who labored in scholastic seclusion. Opposition was strong and widespread, as may have been anticipated by those familiar with the history of the Oxford Movement in England. Some of the early proponents of ritual reform took the position that they were not advocating any doctrinal change, but were concerned only with adiaphora. In other words, they were merely suggesting more meaningful expressions of the faith of the church, a faith which in some respects had become obscured through carelessness, neglect, and false emphases.

The papers read before liturgical institutes of that time abounded in references to the church fathers, the reformers, the Lutheran confessions and the German *Kirchenordnungen* of the post-Reformation period. The writers of these papers were most concerned to establish their orthodoxy, thereby indicating that it was not they, but the contemporary church, which had drifted from its moorings. The inevitable reaction to this toe-treading was often quite loveless. There was much booing and sneering; there was talk of disciplining the innovators. They were called "chancel prancers"—and worse. They did not receive calls, except to other liturgical parishes. They were regarded with suspicion at pastoral conferences. It was fully expected that in time they would become Episcopalians or Roman Catholics.

A few did—and it is to be hoped that they contributed some salutary evangelical emphasis to their new associates. Most, however, endured the insults as best they could, because they were persuaded that the things they stood for would in time be accepted by the church, seeing that essentially the issue revolved around divine truth and beauty. In the following chapter we shall try to estimate the degree to which their program has won acceptance, but at this point let us only say that the liturgical movement has been concerned with something much deeper than adiaphora. Vestments, candles, crucifixes, postures and gestures, liturgies and ceremonies—all such things, as the Augsburg Confession points out, have never been everywhere the same in the church, nor need they be. Behind all these changeable expressions are certain attitudes and emphases—beliefs which have to do with the very heart of the Christian religion.

Therefore, what the proponents of the liturgical movement were really after—and in time the more honest of them came to admit it—was much more than a change in external customs and habits of worship. They wanted to reshape people's religion, people's idea of God, people's attitudes toward the church, the sacraments, and the ministry. Sometimes unconsciously they drove for a very basic alteration in the churchmanship of the time. They stood for worship, adoration, a sense of awe and wonder, of joy and thanksgiving —things which they had lamentably missed in the church in which they had grown up.

Those who were not open to change tried to keep the controversy in the area of adiaphora, and for a while they did. In time, however, the issues became clear, and, while the battleground has shifted in the 60s and 70s, the antagonists are still drawn up along much the same lines. Perhaps it is an oversimplification to say that at bottom the difference was, and remains, between an open and a closed mind, and yet this is surely an important part of it. We must assume, of course, a love for the church in all who are involved. In some this love expresses itself in a fear that, if too much criticism is permitted and too many changes are introduced, the church will no longer be the church—at least not the church in any recognizeable form. In others this love is willing to endure some suffering in its desire to bring about reform of an institution which has become deformed. This was the motivation of Luther and his associates—which is a way of saying that the dominating impulse of the liturgical pioneers was in this same tradition. They felt strongly that a job needed to be done in a church that had fallen into deplorable ways and works. Some of them undoubtedly were "squares" (or "spikes," as the Anglicans call their high-churchmen), but in time the excesses of the early years have levelled off into smoother and more sensible attitudes. Does this mean that the original objectives have been realized, and that historians can label the movement as successful? The answer is both yes and no.

2

MOVING AHEAD:
A PROGRESS REPORT

What has the liturgical movement accomplished? Much in every way.

Architecturally. Completely new styles of church building have been developed. The results in some instances have been curious to behold, but taken as a whole the newer churches are the products of enquiring minds and adventurous spirits; there have been few stereotypes. Contemporary architects have made a fresh approach, an attempt to use designs and materials which above all else are functional and which hopefully are reflective of modern concepts of beauty. It has become quite common, before even thinking of design, for architect and building committee to ask some basic questions concerning the purpose and use of a church building and only then to begin to sketch a structure which might efficiently meet these objectives. In other words, there has been a healthy replacement of traditionalism with honesty. Some contemporary churches are indeed "far out"; this is to be expected in a period of experimentation. Even so, they are signs of life.

Musically. One of the most refreshing developments in modern church life has been the emergence of a whole host of first-rate composers, organists, and choral groups, as well as several organ-builders whose products have given an invaluable assist to the revival of worship. Several publishers have also been most cooperative in promoting this renaissance, and in recent years a new journal called *Church Music* has appeared on the market.

Perhaps the beginnings of this movement may be traced to F. Melius Christiansen, whose St. Olaf Choir became world-famous in the 20s. Since his day several college choirs have gone out into all the earth, singing far better music than was heard at the turn of the century, and, for the most part, doing it much more expertly than their choral predecessors. In some cities local choruses have also done outstanding work, and at least a few congregations have courageously engaged a full-time director of music.

The weak spot in this development is the lamentably deficient program of music in the nation's schools, primary and secondary, public and parochial. One longs for the day when children would be taught to sing, and to enjoy it. As nearly as we can make out, the bottleneck here is in the offices of school administrators. The musicians, bless them, do the best they can—sometimes with a minimum of cooperation. It's difficult to compete with football and basketball.

Artistically. What is most evident to the Sunday worshiper is the evolution of the graphic arts as reflected on the first page of the church bulletin. No longer are visual aids confined to the timeworn symbols; a whole new symbolism is constantly being created on these weekly folders. More permanent is contemporary sacred art in all its forms: painting, needlework, banners, and some statuary, mosaics, and wood-carving. All this has brought color and gaiety to the church. Some of it is baffling to the uninstructed, but, comprehensible or not, it is another sign that something is happening where not much happened before.

Liturgically. The Common Service was constructed on the basis of the consensus of the *Kirchenordnungen* of the 16th century. Since the publication of the *Common Service Book* in 1917 a great deal of liturgical study has been done, and the horizons of the liturgical denominations have been greatly widened. The results of this development were faintly to be discerned in *The Lutheran Hymnal* of 1941, and much more clearly in the 1968 *Service Book and Hymnal*. In the latter volume such refinements as a deacon's litany (extension of the Kyrie), an Old Testament Lesson, and a Eucharistic Prayer were included. The *Worship Supplement* of 1969 carried things a step further by modernizing the Elizabethan pronouns and verb endings, providing two alternate eucharistic liturgies and several additional eucharistic prayers, eliminating the mandatory confession and absolution at the beginning of the service, suggesting variant offertories, general prayers, and post-communion collects. It is evident that for any congregation which makes use of these new materials its liturgy will be both richer and more varied than before. This indeed has been the purpose of the new publications: to provide an opportunity for adventure in worship, so that the church might be delivered from a sterile uniformity and stifling monotony and be introduced to a new spirit of joy and praise.

The same objective lies behind the composition and printing of new musical settings of the liturgy, both those authorized by official commissions of the church and these promoted by independent musicians and publishing houses. There is no lack of opportunity to "sing to the Lord a new song."

Ceremonially. It is sometimes said that people will tolerate liturgical changes much more readily than ceremonial innovations. They will raise little or no objection to recastings of the text, to eliminations, additions, substitutions, and transpositions of what is said or sung, but let some change of action be introduced, and there will be protests aplenty. If therefore there has been acceptance of ceremonial customs suggested by exponents of the liturgical movement, this is very noteworthy. Has there been such acceptance? If by acceptance we mean practice, the answer is that it has been spotty; some congregations have become quite ceremonial, and others are where they were several decades ago.

The growing toleration of so-called "catholic" practices, however, has been most refreshing. People who make the sign of the cross upon themselves at convention services are no longer bombarded with dirty looks and criticizing words. Kneeling for prayer is no longer regarded as an exclusively Roman Catholic posture. Bowing toward the altar is not considered a symptom of incipient idolatry. Some churches are equipped with kneeling benches. Real candles (not fake!) burn at the altar. There may be an eternal light and a paschal candle. A processional cross may be used. An offertory procession is not unknown, nor is a gospel procession. Perhaps laymen will read lessons or suggest subjects for prayer. The clergymen, who used to wear black gown and "beffchen" before they donned surplice and stole, now appear in eucharistic vestments.

All these practices are no longer new, strange

and offensive. Some find them meaningful; others would rather do without them. But the fact that they are tolerated in the church is a definite triumph of the Lutheran principle concerning adiaphora: rites and ceremonies from the historic church should be retained if they are still thought to be useful, but these practices need not be everywhere the same. "It is sufficient for the unity of the church that there be agreement concerning the doctrine of the gospel and the administration of the sacraments."

Organizationally. It was unfortunate that the Lutheran Church—Missouri Synod had no part in the preparation of the *Service Book and Hymnal.* The reasons for this need not be spelled out; that it happened has been regretted by liturgiologists both in the Missouri Synod and the other large Lutheran groups. It looked for awhile as though Mühlenberg's dream of "one church, one book" would not be realized for another generation—the churches which had cooperated in the publication of the *Service Book and Hymnal* would hardly be interested in beginning work on a new, pan-Lutheran volume when the ink on the "old" one was barely dry.

There's no harm in asking, however. So the Missouri Synod evidently thought, for at its 1965 convention, to everyone's surprise, it was resolved "to pursue a cooperative venture with other Lutheran bodies as soon as possible in working toward, under single cover: (a) a common liturgical section in rite, rubric, and music; (b) a common core of hymn texts and musical settings; and (c) a variant selection of hymns if necessary." The American Lutheran Church and Lutheran Church in America readily responded to this invitation, and accordingly the Inter-Lutheran Commission on Worship (ILCW) was formed in 1966. It began to move toward the implementation of its assignment by setting up four committees: on hymn texts, hymn tunes, liturgical texts, and liturgical music.

The first products of these committees have already appeared in print: *Contemporary Worship I—Hymns* (a booklet of 21 hymns) appeared in 1969 and *Contemporary Worship II—Service* in October, 1970. Both booklets are intended to be experimental. They represent a candid attempt to reach out in new directions. Some of the hymns in the first booklet are quite unlike anything presently printed in standard hymnals, and both the liturgical text and the four musical settings of the latter booklet represent a fresh approach to eucharistic worship. A new departure in the liturgical section is the printing of explanations and comments on the pages facing the texts of the service.

The Inter-Lutheran Commission on Worship intends further publications in the same vein: *Contemporary Worship III—Service* (a contemporary musical setting of the *Service Book and Hymnal* rite by Daniel T. Moe) ; *Contemporary Worship IV—Hymns* (a collection of hymns for Baptism, Communion, and confirmation) ; *Contemporary Worship V—Hymns* (collection of sacred folk songs) ; *Contemporary Worship VI— Service* (a service for preaching) . The rites for Holy Baptism, marriage, burial, and confirmation are also being readied. The commission's intention is to solicit reactions from the churches as these materials are put to practical use, so that after sufficient time for testing has elapsed, it will be better informed concerning the direction it is to take. Some of the experimental material will meet with favor, others will not; all of it will be subject to revision. No target date has been set for the publication of the definitive, comprehensive *Service Book and Hymnal,* but some have dared to express the hope that this might coincide with the 400th anniversary of the Book of Concord in 1980.

Ecumenically. In the providence of God, at about the same time that Lutherans were moving toward the greater cooperation just described, those startling developments were taking place in the Roman Catholic church which came to a climax in the second Vatican Council. Liturgical reform was one of the chief concerns of that auspicious meeting. The results have become abundantly evident: free-standing altars, the Mass in the vernacular, new texts for the liturgy, including alternate eucharistic prayers, simplification of ceremonial, a three year cycle of readings, restructuring of the church year, and others. For a while it seemed that the Roman Catholics were on the way to becoming more protestant than the Protestants! On the other hand, ever since the beginnings of the liturgical movement in the Anglican and Lutheran Churches, some of the clergy in these communions had been maintaining positions higher than the normally high church Roman Catholics.

It was time to blow the whistle. The hour had arrived for separated brethren to come together. They were working on the same tasks and were operating with very similar approaches. Their proposals for liturgical reform were often so much alike that liturgies seemed to be almost interchangeable. This has in fact happened, and happened repeatedly; in Lutheran services eucharistic prayers of Roman Catholic origin have been used, as well as liturgies produced by the Taize brethren, the Presbyterian church, and the Commission on Worship of the Consultation on Church Union.

The last mentioned group was the third element in a Consultation on Common Texts formed in 1968, the other two being the ILCW and the Roman Catholics. (The Conference on Church Union in 1968 published its own rite, *An Order of Worship for the Proclamation of the Word of God and the Celebration of the Lord's Supper With Commentary,* in the preparation of which the Rev. Dr. Massey Shepherd played a prominent part.) This group endeavored to arrive at agreed-on versions of liturgical elements in general use in Christian church services: the Our Father, the creeds, the canticles, the chants of the Mass. Its texts of the Our Father and the creeds have been used both in the Consultation on Church Union liturgy and in the *Worship Supplement;* the other items were not complete before the publication of these books.

As the consultation moved toward the completion of its assignment, a more inclusive group, called the International Consultation on English Texts, came into prominence. To the meetings of this group came representatives of various denominations in England, as well as a number of Americans: Dr. Shepherd, Father Gerald Sigler, who was the executive secretary of the Roman Catholic Church's International Commission on English in the Liturgy, and the Rev. Dr. Eugene Brand, representing the ILCW. This group, making good use of the work of the Consultation on Common Texts, has now finished its task, and the results have been published in a pamphlet called *Texts We Have in Common* (Fortress Press, 1970).

The finalized texts in this pamphlet are: the

Lord's Prayer, the Apostles' Creed, the Nicene Creed, the Gloria in Excelsis, the Sanctus and Benedictus, and the Gloria Patri. Provisional texts, on which the consultation is still working, are: Sursum Corda, Agnus Dei, and Te Deum. The American churches might now wish to look at these texts critically to see whether they will be acceptable on this side of the Atlantic. Eventually, of course, each church will have to decide whether it desires to use the texts which will finally be proposed. Even without such final approval, however, progress has already been made toward the elimination of obvious archaisms; some of the new proposals are slowly coming into general use.

Some credit for this inter-denominational activity must be given to the Institute for Liturgical Studies of Valparaiso University. The director of the institute, the Rev. Prof. Hans Boehringer, in 1966 invited representatives of the Roman Catholic, Lutheran, Episcopal, and one or two Protestant churches to come together for an informal consultation to see what might be done on a practical, continuing, cooperative basis. A positive result of this meeting was the Ecumenical Day which was programmed just prior to the Liturgical Weeks of 1967, 1968, and 1969. Perhaps more importantly, the meeting marked the beginning of conversations and friendships which have been mutually helpful. Documents have been interchanged among official commissions, and there has been a voluminous correspondence among the individuals involved. The resultant meeting of minds has been quite striking.

The Institute for Liturgical Studies was founded at Valparaiso in 1949 by Dr. Adolph Wismar, who was ably assisted in the early years by Prof. Van C. Kussrow. It concerned itself at that time with strictly liturgical matters: the structure of the Mass, the apparatus of worship, the lesser services (Matins, Vespers, burial, etc.), posture and gestures, and the like. Many words were written and spoken to advocate the restoration of practices which since the Reformation had fallen into disuse. The best of the essays were published in volumes bearing the title *Pro Ecclesia Lutherana.*

Then, in 1957, the Lutheran World Federation met in Minneapolis, and Valparaiso University took advantage of the presence of prominent European theologians and musicians on this continent; its liturgical and music institutes met simultaneously at Teaneck, New Jersey, and were addressed by a few of the European scholars on their way home. After that meeting the program of the Institute for Liturgical Studies took a definitely doctrinal turn, particularly under the leadership of the Rev. Dr. Robert Schultz. His successor, Prof. Boehringer, has continued this emphasis and has broadened the outreach of the institute to include satellite meetings at St. Olaf College in 1969 and 1970.

Though not primarily concerned with liturgical matters, the Lutheran Society for Worship, Music, and the Arts has, since its foundation in 1958, exerted a powerful influence for good in cultivating good taste in all areas pertaining to the worship of the church. Its chief publication, appropriately entitled *Response,* deserves an *A* rating for good editing and writing. For some years the society, in cooperation with the American Lutheran Church and the Lutheran Church-Missouri Synod, sponsored a series of summer institutes for church musicians and clergymen. Its mimeographed bibliographies and reference guides have also been useful.

Sacramentally. The most consistent emphasis of the liturgical movement in all effected denominations has been on the Sacrament of the Altar. Indeed, so much has been said about the proper place of Holy Communion in the life of the church that it is difficult to summarize. But the following notes have constantly been struck:

1. There should be more frequent celebrations of Holy Communion; the sacrament should become central and prominent in the devotional life of the church. In the Lutheran church this repeated emphasis has produced results: weekly celebrations in city churches have become the

rule; in others the four-times-a-year practice of the 30s has been increased to once a month.

2. The faithful should be urged to receive the sacrament more frequently; preachers should emphasize its blessing and its rightful use. This plea likewise has affected a steady increase in the number of communions per member per year, from a low of two and one-half at the close of the 30s to an average of about five and three-fourths in 1969.

3. The mood in which the celebration is conducted should be one of praise and thanksgiving; the eucharistic note should be loud and clear. Gradually this too has "caught on," as the faithful have learned to think of the period of worship as a happy time, a wedding feast, an hour of fulfillment in which God's people rejoice in fellowship with him and with one another.

4. The meal aspect should be brought into prominence: the family gathered around the table in the Father's house, sharing the food which he provides. Where this has been emphasized, eucharistic services have lost much of their starchiness and in some parishes have become quite informal.

The Heart of the Matter. Much of what has been said in this chapter has to do with externals, with customs, techniques, statistics, books, vestments, and church buildings. All this striving for proper expression is no doubt well and good; but has it reached down into the interior life of the members of the church? Are people today more skilled worshipers because of these developments, better informed, more intense, more devoted, more transformed? Is the church stronger today because of the liturgical movement? It is impossible to answer the question with accuracy; the spiritual life of a Christian is not capable of measurement. All we can do is to point to trends, signs, and symptoms. These are sure to be spotty and irregular; what will be true of one church body, area, parish, or person will not be true of others. Generalizations are especially risky here, but a few estimates may nevertheless be ventured.

1. We've come a long way. Since Luther D. Reed began his pioneering work in the first quarter of the century, since the activity of the Liturgical Society of St. James in the second quarter (the names of Wismar, Von Schenk, and Bergen come particularly to mind), since the beginning of the wedding of liturgy and doctrine in the 50s, and the ecumenical activity of the 60s, there have been notable advances in the art of worship. It would be strange indeed if the new spirit did not infect altar guilds, choirs, schools, and a host of individuals who have been caught up in the drive for renewal. Some camp-followers along the way have become bogged down in

antiquarianism or formalism, but far more people have understood the objectives and in their own ways have striven for realization of the same. There can be little doubt that progress has been made.

2. A great enrichment has taken place in liturgy, ceremony, and all the ecclesiastical arts. The church today is equipped with a far better arsenal of the implements of worship. Here again, it is difficult to suppose that all these new contributions from many sources have had zero effect on either clergy or laity. The contemporary liturgical atmosphere is quite different from that of a half century ago, and so are the people who breathe it.

3. We have experienced a notable broadening in our concept of the church. We have become aware of the ways of worship in the Orthodox church. We have seen lines of thought converging among liturgiologists in various branches of the western church—a phenomenon which has led to the publication of *Studia Liturgica,* an international, interdenominational journal, and to the more recent formation of *Societas Liturgica,* a comprehensive fellowship of liturgical scholars. We have come to see that the possibilities of meeting on this level are much more promising than on the ground of minutely particularized doctrinal agreement. So, as we have learned from one

another through repeated personal contact, the thing we had suspected from the beginning has become experientially clear: The church is one, and the closer its people get to the Lord, the closer they get to one another. It's a great joy to discover brothers and sisters in other denominations. There may be "diversities of operations and differences of administrations," but it is the same Spirit who works in all of God's children. The problem of inter-communion is not solved as yet, but it appears by no means as insoluble as it did 30 years ago.

This brings us to the contemporary scene. What do things look like today, and what is the prognosis?

3

THE NEW MOOD

It is ironical that the Inter-Lutheran Commission on Worship (ILCW), which was organized for the expressed purpose of producing a service book and hymnal common to all English-speaking Lutheran churches on this continent, should find itself momentarily unable to do so. If the task were to put together a volume which would be agreeable to all the various cultural traditions, ethnic groups, and social classes to be found in contemporary Lutheranism, this would be difficult, but not impossible.

A New World

But the problem confronting the ILCW goes much deeper than that. It is related to the upheaval of our whole society, the bewildering revolution of our morals and manners, our speech and our conduct, our entire way of living. Basic to all this is our religious faith. Few of us believe in God in the same way that we did two or three decades ago—a development partially due, of course, to our spiritual maturation, which presumably would have taken place in any event, but more profoundly to the changed world of the atomic age. Everything is different from what it used to be—which means that we are different too, affecting and being affected by our environment to a degree which was utterly impossible in the pre-scientific era. We think, speak, and act differently—and we believe differently, too. Even a superficial contact with the thought-patterns of the Middle Ages will make it clear how profoundly present-day Christianity has changed: Churches that have clung to medieval customs have been forced to make a choice between giving up these traditions or becoming completely irrelevant. The Roman Catholic church's surrender of Latin to the vernacular is perhaps the most obvious example of this.

There are others. One is the simplification of ceremony in the Roman Catholic Mass. Present rubrics call for fewer genuflections, signs of the cross, and movements from place to place. Bishops wear less expensive vestments, women are no longer required to wear headgear in church, and the introduction of lay commentary, offertory processions, and hymnody has created a markedly less formal atmosphere in the congregation. A frequent explanation of this development is that much of the ceremonial we have inherited was first introduced in the church as an aping of court procedure, or at any rate was a reflection of a society in which great deference was paid to emperors and kings, dukes, lords, and earls. Since we live in a democratic world today, this repeated bowing and scraping is foreign to our approach and should therefore be eliminated. So runs the argument, and it seems reasonable enough. However, the old danger of extremism lurks in it, as the following incident may illustrate.

At a Roman Catholic seminary recently a Mass was said in which, from start to finish, the congregation did not once make use of the kneeling benches. On the other hand, the worshipers (mostly seminary students) participated freely in an informal discussion of a playlet which had been presented in the chancel. Guitars and drums led the singing of folk songs. All this gave visitors the strong impression that what was going on was entirely an expression of a horizontal relationship; there was little of the vertical dimension. The worship of a transcendent God seemed lacking; the absence of moments of adoration indicated, very disturbingly, that perhaps the congregation felt that there was no one to adore. A conversation with a few of the students after the Mass strengthened this impression. One of them said that everything that could be known of God was communicated through other people, that God was to be discovered only in one's fellowman, that he was not to be thought of as a being separate from his people. Therefore, continued this student, a church service should be an expression of the church as the body of Christ, that is, the members of that body should relate to one another as such, sharing with one another whatever spiritual gifts they enjoyed, and so experiencing the richness of the fellowship of the Holy Spirit.

The last sentence is true enough; the preceding one is indeed an extremist point of view. One can well understand it as a reaction against the individualistic worship of former times, in which —especially in the great cathedrals—there was a great deal of awesomeness, perhaps mingled with a bit of superstition. Now mystery and miracle are downgraded. What the priest does at the altar he does facing the people, in the sight of all. Choirs and organs have been muted, and the people swing and sway to rock music. Not much adoration is left; the transcendent God has been largely replaced by an immanent one. The mood of worship has changed. It used to be a worshipful concentration on him who was thought to be wholly other; now it is joyful praise to the God who is in the midst of his people. The shift has been profound; it is not just a difference in sight and sound. In many lives one's concept of God has undergone a radical transformation.

The danger of extremism appears in the seminarian's point of view, which is really heretical. Denial of God as a person—to say nothing of three persons—is theologically reprehensible. This rules out any one-to-one or group-to-one relationship to him. It eliminates prayer. There is no longer any focal point in worship; there is only group activity. Finally, in such a religion, there is no divine mind, no paternal solicitude, no wise providence, no personal intervention into the ordinary course of cause and effect, no being to appeal to in time of trouble or to praise for exceptional blessing. The kind of worship common to the church since the beginning—indeed, the kind practiced by God's people in Old Testament times —has disappeared. What is far worse, the God who is the Father of our Lord Jesus has been dethroned.

In restyling church ceremonial we who are members of official commissions and committees must be aware of what we are doing; we must not be so zealous for innovation that we lose our central values. The new emphasis on the meal, the family, the joy of the people of God is a refreshing change from the funereal gloom which used to characterize many church services. But this must be kept in balance with a profound adoration of the transcendent being who remains the object of all worship. Lutherans in time past have experienced great difficulty in cultivating and capturing this atmosphere of awe and wonder. They have emphasized the preaching of the Word, which often meant a heavy emphasis on pedagogy. They have been afraid of anything smacking of mysticism—perhaps because of Luther's tussles with the *Schwärmer*. As a result, most Lutheran services are run-of-the-mill, routine performances of a liturgy which has lost its meaning for most of the congregation. The faithful have no opportunity for personal prayer, or, if they do, are too self-conscious to take advantage of it. Indeed, very few people have advanced beyond the kindergarten stage in the art of prayer.

Function and Forms

Is it functional?—no more penetrating question could be asked concerning anything that is done in church. And it is a question which should be asked insistently, because we stand in perennial danger of either continuing to do things which have lost their significance, or neglecting to do what could be of great significance for us: sins of commission or omission. Three examples of functionality—or the lack of it—may be adduced from the Lutheran liturgy.

The first is that of the introit. The introit is supposed to be an entrance song, and it is so labelled in English missals published within the Roman Catholic church. This was its ancient significance; it was an entire psalm, buttressed fore and aft with an antiphon, which was sung in days of yore as the reverend clergy made their way into the church to begin the service. But it is very evident that the introit in our Lutheran services no longer fulfills this function, since the minister has entered the sanctuary at least five minutes before that point is reached. A hymn has been sung (is this the modern entrance song?) and the confession and absolution have been spoken; why do we any longer think about an entrance?

We may indeed think about a beginning, since what has already transpired has been definitely preparatory in nature, but in that event let us stop talking about an introit and call it a theme or keynote, or something of the sort; and let us choose psalm verses with this in mind. On the other hand, if we are to continue to operate with the introit concept, there should be an actual entrance of the clergy at this point, and the service should be so constructed as to make this feasible. Perhaps the best suggestion would be to divorce the confession and absolution from the service itself, with an interlude or a period of silence in between, during which the ministers might put on their vestments and then come into the sanctuary as the introit is sung.

Another possibility might be substituting hymns for the traditional introit. This has something to recommend it, and that something is congregational participation. Surely this is one of the prime objectives of the liturgical movement: the greater involvement of the people of God in their priestly functions. It is almost necessary, however, that the introits be sung by a choir or cantor; for the celebrant to sing them would be somewhat analogous to a bride sitting at a portable organ sliding down the center aisle playing Lohengrin; and for him to speak the words is hardly any better. If there is neither choir nor cantor, one must fall back on the congregation; and most congregations would find this a formidable assignment. It would, however, be possible for the people to sing a hymn. Why not?

The best answer—and perhaps the only one— is that in singing man-made hymns the church gets away from the inspired words of Scripture. The psalms become even more unknown than they are now, and the substituted hymns may not always be appropriate, since the choice of these would be left to the pastor, and he—if one may be pardoned for saying so—may not have the best taste in the world. To retain the introits would mean eliminating the truly soul-shaking possibility of inserting somewhat ghastly spiritual songs here.

There are arguments on both sides. Perhaps the best solution, as has been indicated, lies in a thorough revision of the present series of introits, so that they would be chosen with some view of harmonizing with the rest of the propers for the day. That, coupled with a restoration of the entrance procession, would solve the problem.

Much the same things as have been said about the introit might be repeated concerning the gradual. The gradual is supposed to be a transition piece between Epistle and Gospel, and some have said that the first part of it is intended to reflect the teaching of the Epistle, while the latter part forecasts the Gospel. At best this is only half correct, since, as nearly as we can make out, the verses which now appear before the Alleluia or Tract were originally chanted between the Old Testament Lesson and the Epistle, while the remainder (Alleluia Verse or Tract) was sung in anticipation of the Gospel. When the Old Testament Lesson was dropped from the liturgy, all of this was fused together into what we now call the gradual. The Old Testament Lesson has been restored in *Service Book and Hymnal,* and in the new service book of the future the present graduals may be split into the original component parts.

This, however, would not penetrate to the nub of the problem, which is to make the gradual a really functional part of the service. To do this two steps would be helpful. First, the texts should be revised to harmonize with the lessons. Obviously, this was not done when the present texts were selected: Scriptural texts were simply chosen in canonical order, the only point being to sing some verses from the psalms. But relevant texts can be found and used, as may be demonstrated from the graduals of the major festivals. It is a project which cries out to be undertaken.

Another suggestion comes under the heading of ceremonial, and will therefore encounter greater resistance. This is a restoration of the gospel procession, at least on the more important days of the calendar. Before hackles start to rise, let us consider first of all that as Lutherans we believe in the real presence of Christ, not only in the sacrament, but also in the Word. This means that when the Word is read in church, it is not only words about the Word, but the Word himself which is being uttered. The Gospel in a special way is that Word, since it is the record of the words and deeds of our Lord. When therefore the Gospel is read, this is to be regarded as Christ himself speaking to his people here and now. Out of respect for him who so speaks, the congregation rises, and when the reading is finished, the people don't say, "Thanks, pastor, for reading this to us," but, "Praise be to Thee, O Christ," since it is he whose word they have just heard.

It would be quite in keeping with the doctrine of the real presence in the Word for the gospeller to proceed to a unique place in the church to read this Word. It would furthermore be meaningful if this place were close to, or even in the midst of the people, since the mandate of the church is to preach the gospel to people, that is, to go where the people are and to cause them to hear the Word of Jesus Christ. Since this is a large part of the reason for our existence, its importance could well be visibly demonstrated by a gospel procession. If this were done, the Alleluia would take an added significance, being sung as the procession moved toward the people.

The ushers' march forward with the offering plates is a miserable remnant of a third procession that deserves to be restored. This is the offertory procession. Before we discuss the procession itself, however, we should consider where we are in the service. The preacher's pax at the end of the sermon marks the end of the office of the Word; the rest of the service is occupied with the office of the sacrament. This means that the singing of an offertory at a service which is not a celebration of Holy Communion (for example, the liturgy beginning on page 5 of *The Lutheran Hymnal*) is out of place. One of the unfortunate results of this practice has been that people have almost universally thought of the offertory as a sort of appendage to the sermon, a welcome chance for a seventh inning stretch after the preacher's lengthy utterance. The editors of the *Service Book and Hymnal* have sought to correct this by specifying that the offertory is to be sung only after the offerings have been received and at the time when they are brought forward. This is commendable, and so is the inclusion of two additional offertory texts, one of which is especially appropriate: "What shall I render to the Lord for all his benefits toward me? I will take the cup of salvation and call upon the name of the Lord. . . ."

We should now take a further step, one which will bring out the full significance of the offertory action: the presentation at the altar of the gifts of bread and wine by certain representatives of the people of God. To spell out the doctrinal overtones of this movement is beyond the scope of this chapter—suffice it to say that these products of man's time and energy, as well as of God's munificence, are here offered to God partly as a token and partly as a response to a specific command. They are a token which implies that not only these things, but all products of our time and energy ought to be put into the service of the Lord; indeed, our whole selves ought so to be offered, as we express it in one of the general prayers of the church.

The bread and wine are also presented before the altar in response to the specific command of Christ, a command which, as our Anglican friends keep reminding us, involves the fourfold action of taking (offertory), blessing (consecration),

53

breaking (fraction), and giving (sharing—the distribution). Unless then the bread and wine are deliberately brought to the altar at the time of the offertory, the liturgical significance of this chant is lost.

One way of doing this, of course, is tradition: allowing the bread and wine to rest on a credence table, and then transferring them to the altar at the offertory. But a better method is to choose two people from the congregation to come down the center aisle with the ushers, so that the entire offering—money, bread, wine, prayers, and self—may be brought before the Lord at the same time.

At these three points in the service, there might well be a restoration of ceremonial: introit, gospel, and offertory. To be consistent about it, we should either restore the three processions or eliminate the three liturgical chants. If the chants are to be retained, their texts should undergo thorough review and radical revision. To substitute hymns at this point would be a second-best alternative.

A Movement of the Whole Person

Ceremonial invariably involves movement, and spells activity. If one thinks of the liturgy as "the people's work," not only the officiating ministers, but all the faithful should be active in worship. Here Kirkegaard's famous illustration of a theater is in point. He said that for the congregation to think of itself as an audience witnessing the performance of the clergy and listening critically to the music of choir and organ is all wrong. God himself is the audience, watching the performance of his people; as for the ministers and musicians, they are merely the prompters helping the people to do their job well. A proper performance does not consist merely in speaking certain lines, but of fitting action to the words. This means that a worshiper must not only have memorized the text, but also understand what postures, gestures, and movements will make the text most meaningful. It's like being at a formal dinner: one should know both how to make polite conversation and what implements to use while eating.

This may sound as though Christian worship is a rigid adherence to a prescribed protocol, so that anyone making a mistake should feel guilty of an unpardonable breech of etiquette. Actually it is not that way at all. There are of course certain customs and practices which are generally accepted in the church, and worshipers ought to be well-briefed about these, so that is not necessary for the officiant to tell them when to stand, sit, or kneel, when to bow, make the sign of the cross, or say amen.

Once these standard procedures have been mastered, however, a worshiper should lose all self-consciousness and participate in the liturgy easily and naturally. He will be at home. Variations in liturgy or music will not throw him for a loss for he will accept the fact that while there is a framework, a skeletal liturgy which is universal, all sorts of variants are possible. In fact, the variations are quite necessary to the life of the church, since without them corporate worship can quickly become stagnant. The drive for renewal in worship has as its constant objective that the faithful will "come alive," finding worship to be an ongoing pageant of adventure. In this an open-minded worshiper learns to participate with eagerness and excitement.

Psychologists have been telling us for some time past that a man is not a tripartite organism, easily divided into body, mind, and spirit; but a unified whole, so that whatever he does both expresses his entire personality and makes an inverse impression on him. The application of this principle to worship is that the body can by no means be divorced from the action, as though a man could worship with his mind only or with his spirit only, or with both together, the body being isolated from the experience in any event. Perhaps behind such a notion is the ancient idea that the body is something evil, and therefore can have no part in human fellowship with God; one must strive for escape from physical limitations, so that the soul may be free to enter into communion with the deity. This is neither good theology nor sound psychology. A Christian's body, says St. Paul, is a temple of the Holy Spirit, and so plays its part in the worship of God. To confine one's spiritual life to intellectual exercise or unmoving meditation is to stunt one's growth. A full-orbed act of worship calls for expression from the voice, ears, eyes, hands, knees, and feet. The whole person exists for the service of the Lord, and the church is the place for this to be acknowledged by the surrender of one's entire being to the Christ who sacrificed himself completely on the cross and now lives as the Lord of all life.

4

SPEAKING OF GOD

In our time-minded, high-pressured, and impatient age we are not interested in obscurity. Machines must be efficient, clothes must be functional (and minimal!), furniture must fulfill the purpose for which it has been designed. We moderns are not distinguished for our elegance; indeed we have a strong suspicion that elegance conceals more than it reveals, and we scorn concealment. "Tell it like it is!" is the insistent demand of the "now" generation—a watchword that seems deliberately ungrammatical to draw attention to itself. We are summoned to a vigorous honesty; to young people, "phoniness" is a repulsive disease. This being so, it would seem that of all places where strict honesty is in order the Christian church should be pre-eminent, for Christians put their faith in one who said, "I am the truth."

The church's stock-in-trade is words. Some of

these words are variable; in liturgical language we call them "the propers." Other elements in the liturgy are always the same, and to them particular attention must be paid, for these are words which must wear well. The simplest of these responses may be the most difficult to revise when some updating of language is undertaken. What shall we substitute for "and with thy spirit"—which is a patently archaic expression? "And with you too"? "And also with you"? "And with you as well"? Nothing sounds completely adequate, possibly because we are so accustomed to the old that anything new sounds a bit jarring.

How about "it is meet, right, and salutary"? Two words in this ought to be changed, but what do we come up with? "It is right and proper"? "It is right and just"? "It is our duty and our delight"? Shall we get rid of "Hosanna" in the Sanctus? How about the word "hosts" in the same chant? "World without end" at the conclusion of the Gloria Patri and the collects does not convey much meaning to the modern ear. The first line of the Gloria in Excelsis is a major problem, although here the difficulty is as much exegetical as it is linguistic. In "he descended into hell" a dogmatic question is involved. There has been great uncertainty about how to retranslate "and lead us not into temptation," and in Lutheran circles there has been some bridling over the use of the word "catholic" in the creeds. These examples illustrate the difficulty of finding the right words, and the still greater difficulty of getting churches to agree on texts to be used in the liturgy.

Common Texts

Why should such an attempt be made at all? There are several reasons: (1) Since the need for modernization is obvious, it is reasonable to enlist the services of those best qualified to undertake it, regardless of their denominational tags. (2) The Christian family ought to speak the same language; this seems incontrovertible. (3) In this era of ecumenism there are many occasions on which Christians of various denominations come together and join in some act of corporate worship, be it no more than saying the Our Father in unison. The same need for agreement in text arises in mixed-marriage homes. Likewise, our frequent moving about, both on holidays and in change of residence, calls for the same agreement. Why can't Christians feel at home, at least to this extent, wherever they go in the Christian community? (4) It would be very helpful for musicians to have standard texts to use when they undertake to compose new settings. Their compositions could then be used in any liturgical church without the slightest feeling of foreignness; for example, Lutherans would no longer feel that somebody had tampered with the text when they hear, "Glory be to thee, O Lord most high" instead of "Hosanna in the highest."

Some of the work of revision is very easy. It is not difficult, for instance, to change the Elizabethan personal pronouns to modern usage; the problem for the ordinary worshiper is to become adjusted to saying "You" to God. And this illustrates the major difficulty in this whole business: the painful surrender of time-hallowed church usage and long-term personal habit to new expressions and customs which, however reasonable they may be, are nevertheless strange and therefore unwelcome. The current restiveness about liturgical change was inevitable; it was also necessary if any improvement was to be made. One only hopes that it will be quite temporary. A cliche among advertisers is that when a new thing is offered, the public first abhors, then tolerates, and finally embraces it. Perhaps we are now in the second phase of liturgical change: toleration. Shall we presently embrace the new things?

We must, of course, face up to the disquieting possibility that the situation will never become settled, that we shall not again have a liturgy which is accepted always, everywhere, and by all people. The Roman Catholic Mass used to be like that. It is not likely it will ever be so again. The barriers of language will prevent this, but beyond that, the variations now permitted, for example, in the choice of eucharistic prayers, will

61

make impossible a return to the stereotyped kind of worship that prevailed everywhere before Vatican II.

In the Lutheran church, too, a considerable variety in liturgical usage does and will continue to exist. This, however, is of a somewhat different stamp than it used to be. Variety has now become an accepted principle in the official commissions of the church. In the *Worship Supplement* no less than five eucharistic prayers are to be found. The ILCW's *Contemporary Worship II—Service,* beside introducing a new liturgy, offers four widely differing musical settings. Do not such publications create a chaotic situation in the church, a liturgical confusion far worse than before? Don't they work at cross-purposes with the movement which seeks agreement in liturgical texts? Doesn't the ILCW defeat its own purpose, which is precisely the unification of worship practices in the English-speaking Lutheran church?

It may seem so; but it must be borne in mind that these publications are not intended to be definitive. They are frankly tentative, experimental. In a time of revolution they are testings to determine how far the church wishes the liturgical revolution to proceed. The hope of the ILCW is that there will be sufficient feedback from those using the new materials to give it a clear indication of how to proceed—at least a clearer sign than it has at the present moment. The commission remains conscious of its mandate to produce a permanent (as much as any service book and hymnal can be) volume.

But what if the results of this experimentation are not conclusive? What if no definite pattern emerges? Can we adjust to the possibility that from here on in there will be no common service, no universally used musical setting? This development has already begun: three musical settings of the "old" liturgy have the approval of the Commission on Worship of the LC-MS, two orders appear in *Service Book and Hymnal* and one other as a separate pamphlet, another is to be found in the *Worship Supplement,* and four more (of the new liturgy) in *Contemporary Worship II— Service.* Two variant eucharistic liturgies are printed in the *Worship Supplement,* and the order in *Contemporary Worship II—Service* is still another. Is this trend to continue? Will people ever again be able to feel at home with what goes on in church?

The Unifying Core

Admittedly some adjustment is required of the faithful. But it is not so great as may be anticipated. Any Christian liturgy we have ever seen, as long as it attempts to use Word and Sacrament in the same service, follows a basic plan. The first part of the service consists of Bible readings followed by some sort of commentary, and the second part consists of the meal which usually, though sometimes obscurely, consists of the fourfold action of taking (offertory), thanking (eucharistic prayer), breaking (fraction), and sharing (communion). Knowledge of this basic skeleton of the service should enable the worshiper to follow any liturgy, regardless of the language used to express these ideas. When the action is sacramental (Bible readings, sermon), he should experience no difficulty whatsoever; but what of the sacrificial elements, in which he is expected to participate verbally and by bodily movement?

These things must be indicated on either printed or mimeographed page, and it is to be anticipated that some variety will be encountered here. But this too should not prove an insurmountable obstacle: the text and the directions for worship will always be spelled out, and the structure, the thought progression, the climactic order, will always be the same. Once the worshiper becomes accustomed to the idea of variety, he will discover to his relief that the variety consists only in the expression of the great ideas of the liturgy, not the ideas themselves. The church, after all, is always the same; it's just her garments that are fashionable.

The musical problem is more difficult. All that we know for sure is that the church dare not confine herself to one setting of the liturgy. Where this is done, formalism fastens its icy fingers on the faithful. If this is doubted, we suggest that the congregation be asked some Sunday to speak the liturgy. The result, we predict, will be embarrassing—even disastrous. It will become painfully evident that not only have the people not been thinking of what they have been singing, but that they don't even know the words! The music, which is supposed to illuminate the text, has in time come to conceal it! A different setting hopefully will inject new life and meaning into the old rite. If this is to happen, all concerned will have to overcome a strong tendency to inertia. Pastor, musician, and congregation will have to exert themselves to learn the new setting, and everyone will have to be both open to the change and patient, very patient, in assimilating it. Is it worth the trouble, worth the possible "turning off" of those who are not open to change? We think it is. Anything is preferable to grinding through the same chants Sunday after Sunday, year after year, *ad infinitum, ad nauseam*. What we are after—or should be—is renewal.

Elegance vs. Clarity

Let us return to the problem of language. This is not only a matter of changing the personal pronouns and archaic verb endings, but of adopting a different stylistic prose. It is said of Archbishop

Cranmer—whose texts are scattered all through our "old" Lutheran liturgy—that he never used one adjective where two would do. This is no joke—he really did. It was the fashion of the time, the style of elegance in an age when Englishmen were almost intoxicated with the possibilities of a language come of age. Writers of that time were enamored of the principle of "two for one," which is illustrated in our collects. Here are a few examples, taken at random, of the balance of one word or phrase over against another: "That they may both perceive and know what things they ought to do and also may have grace and power faithfully to fulfill the same;" "Keep us both outwardly and inwardly that we may be defended from all adversities which may happen to the body and from all evil thoughts which may assault and hurt the soul;" "That they may love what thou commandest and desire what thou dost promise;" "pure and clear;" "protect and comfort;" "virtuous and godly." Without doubt this is beautiful language. It cannot be surpassed for its rhythm and cadence.

The same thing can be said of the King James Version of the Bible, which was made in about the same period. It is not being used much any more, not because it has lost its beauty, but because its elegance—to say nothing of its archaisms—often conceals rather than reveals the meaning. Many of us have reluctantly laid the King James

Version aside and have begun to use the Revised Standard, Phillips, or the New English Bible. There is no question that these speak the Word to us more penetratingly than a text 350 years old.

Likewise, preachers today do not talk like the church fathers, or like Luther, or even like Spurgeon; if they do, nobody listens. Unless they use speech that is "understanded of the people," they might just as well not say anything. The same principle applies to the liturgy. Many of us harbor a nostalgia for Cranmerian language, but we must accept the fact that this is no longer the idiom, and that those who continue to use the archaic forms will only strengthen the impression that religion is divorced from life, that what we say in church has nothing to do with what we say and do the rest of the time.

The new liturgical language is therefore more direct and streamlined, less wordy and elaborate. Sometimes the results are bumpy and abrupt; our generation has not yet produced a Cranmer. But this is one of the things which simply has to be endured by people who live in a time of transition. After a while, no doubt, the rough places will be made plain and the crooked straight. At the moment we are chiefly interested in saying what we mean.

Some find such straightforward language offensive. They have a deep-seated feeling that God should be addressed in words that are different and more "exalted" than the words we use in speaking to one another. And this is so, they say, because of the gap that exists between us and God —because he is "wholly other," because his "judgments are unsearchable and his ways past finding out." Since he is holy and we are not, he must be approached with the utmost reverence, and the language of our prayers ought to express this.

With much of this sentiment we have a good deal of sympathy. Sectarian worship which seems to treat God as though he were a brother Rotarian to be slapped on the back and acclaimed as a jolly good fellow—this to us, who have been trained in some sort of liturgical tradition, seems vulgar and indecent. Our predilection for stateliness must, however, be qualified by one thing: the fact of the incarnation. Since the birth of Christ no man has been able rightly to say that God has remained utterly inscrutable. Rather, in the advent of his Son he has bridged the gap and joined himself to our condition in a marvelous condescension. This does not mean that he can now be dealt with like one of us, in the sense of being our equal. But it does mean that he is profoundly interested in establishing communication on our own level, speaking to us through the voice of a man, sacrificing a body and a spirit like ours. Down through the centuries the faithful have knelt or bowed in great awe at the words of the creed, "and was incarnate by the Holy Ghost of the Virgin Mary, and was made man."

Our liturgical speech, therefore, is quite different from what it would have been if Christ had not come. It is still cast in the mood of adoration, but the adoration is now saturated with a joyful thanksgiving. Indeed, the adoration is far deeper because of Christ; we now have *that* reason for thinking highly of God. There are of course times and places for penitence and for meditating on the grim facts of death and judgment. But these are not the dominant characteristics of Christian prayer; this is not the keynote of the liturgy. When redeemed children of God come together, their overriding purpose is to express their gladness in being members of his family. This is a two-directional relationship, as a Post-Communion collect expresses it when it talks about "faith toward thee and perfect love toward one another." In neither direction should there be any barriers. We are "one body in Christ and members one of another."

"The fruit of the Spirit is love, joy, and peace," and this should be evident in a superlative degree in corporate worship. This is why a guitar mass or folk service appeals to the young in spirit: somehow in these circumstances the spiritual fruit seems to burst forth as the faithful are moved to shed some of their usual reserve. We shall come back to this in a later chapter—the point at the

69

moment is that this same child-like unaffectedness might well be expressed in the phraseology of our liturgy. If it is, the liturgy will be quite different from the courtly language of our ancestors. Perhaps that is not to be regretted too much. If the Spirit has his way with us, it's all to the good.

The drive for clarity and honesty in liturgical language finds strong support in modern translations of the Bible. Again and again, as the new versions have appeared, we have found passages to be startlingly pointed which previously had been obscured by outdated words. It has become evident that the Holy Spirit never intended his meaning to be beclouded by polite circumlocutions or meaningless metaphors. Liturgiologists might well take their cure from this as they set about producing texts in the language of today. Language changes rapidly, but that fact has not deterred the translators from doing their work, any more than it prevented the prophets and apostles from writing the books of the Bible in the first place. No doubt the revisions, because of the faster rate of change today, will have to be more frequent than they used to be. But this is our task, to be undertaken with as much wisdom and skill as is available to us. It must be pursued with one eye on the unchanging reality on which our faith is built, and the other on a world which moves with bewildering rapidity.

5

GUITARS AND CELLS:
NEW LIFE FOR THE PARISH

We have been assuming that as we seek to reform the liturgy, the political structure of the
church will remain what it is today. Perhaps this
has been too glib an assumption; there are a lot
of voices warning of immanent change. Dozens
of books and articles have appeared prophesying
the demise of the parish, or at least urging a radical overhauling of the parochial system. Behind
these lugubrious judgments on contemporary
church life lies a great weariness with the *kaffee-
klatsches* of women's groups, the wiener roasts of
young people, the men's dartball leagues—and also
the more basic organizational structure of a congregation: its budgets and financial campaigns,
its building programs, its priviledged position as
a tax-exempt corporation. Critics of all this point
out that the early church was spectacularly success-

ful without any of this, while we, with all our modern business techniques, are steadily losing ground. What is needed, they say, is not more efficiency, but more of the Holy Spirit; not better organization, but more involved and devoted Christians.

The question is, how can such Christians be produced? A widely-given answer rests on the presupposition that many of our congregations are too large for an individual to find self-realization. He gets lost in the crowd. He becomes a number on the books of the financial secretary, a card in the communicants' file. If he is absent from church for a while, nobody notices it—perhaps not even the pastor. He can get married or divorced or promoted or discharged without a flicker of interest from any fellow member. He can be a man whom nobody knows, especially if he is a shy sort of person. He doesn't feel needed, and after a while doesn't feel wanted.

Worship and Music

There are, however, certain values attached to a large congregation—values which hopefully would not be lost in whatever reorganization of the church might take place. One of these is the strength that is imparted by being in a great company of fellow-believers. This is by no means to be written off as though it were nothing more than a pride in numbers or mere crowd psychology. The church is veritably "a great multitude which no man can number," and the triumphant section of it, as depicted in the last book of the Bible, is engaged in an act of corporate worship that is utterly magnificent. In our present situation, with our limited facilities and our sinful natures, we cannot hope to duplicate the adoration of the saints in glory; but we ought to make the attempt. Maybe we might call it choir practice, a getting into condition for the time when we shall join the heavenly chorus. In any cvcnt, it's all one church: the church triumphant and the church expectant, and it would appear that the latter division of it should approximate, as closely as possible, the worship of the former. There are occasions when we seem to come close. There are times when the sheer power of thousands of voices gives us a foretaste of our promised experience in the life of the world to come.

Our present experience almost invariably has musical accompaniment. Music is exceedingly important to worship—which brings up the perennial question of what kind of music is to be played and sung, and what instruments are to be used in church. All we can do here is to voice our opinion, in the full realization that there will be widespread disagreement.

Guitar masses and folk music services are attempts to make the individual worshipers, particularly those who usually feel excluded, more at home. The designation "folk music" indicates this. If the music is popular, down to earth, easily learned and sung, everybody should feel comfortable with it. And in those parishes where services of this kind have been introduced, there is no doubt that all present are much more relaxed than they usually are in church. The very novelty of the service, the simplicity of the music, and the informality of the musicians does effectively penetrate the bored rigidity of the usual Sunday congregation, bringing about a release of joy that is a refreshment to all who are open to receive it. Perhaps for the first time in their lives, members clap their hands in church and seem genuinely happy to be there. They rejoice in the presence of their fellow members and demonstrate this at the greeting of peace. They participate in the service with a new enthusiasm. Once again the church seems to come alive.

On the other hand, when it is all over, people frequently say, "I enjoyed this very much, but I wouldn't want to do it every Sunday." This qualification indicates a widespread recognition that folk music, while easy to sing and rhythmically infectious, does not have good wearing quality. Fed a steady diet of it, the faithful might soon tire of it and might cast about for something new to take its place. Their feeling would probably include the guitar also, for the guitar is not the most versatile instrument in the world. Its capabilities are quite limited, and congregations whose singing would be led every Sunday exclusively by guitarists might soon scream for relief.

We keep thinking, however, of how a congregation can be stimulated by this type of music; it's a value which shouldn't be minimized and which the church can hardly afford to lose. We have had far too little love, joy, and peace in time past; somehow now, since these fruits have begun to blossom, the soil in which they grow must be carefully cultivated. What does that mean?

Several things come to mind. One of these is that the church needs to pay much more attention to music than it has in the past. The success of folk music services demonstrates how vital it is to permit Christians to express themselves in ways which they find congenial. This does not mean that church music should be no better than the least common denominator of public taste—rather, that it should not be confined to one idiom. The chorales are great, but one may grow weary of them also unless hymns from other traditions are interjected. The church, being catholic, includes people of diverse musical tastes. The practices that they find congenial may vary widely. This must be borne in mind in the selection of hymns and the planning of the services.

Variety is the key to the situation, a variety which is cognizant of the choral limitations of the congregation but which nevertheless seeks to enlarge its repertoire. If this is to happen, new material will repeatedly have to be introduced. As far as hymns are concerned, this should not be too difficult, provided the music is not utterly impossible. Liturgical music is something else again, unless it is music which makes use of familiar melodies. To teach a congregation a new mass, like Willan's or Bender's or Moe's or Bunjes-Hillert's, is a major undertaking, requiring months of after-service rehearsals and perhaps a few years of "getting with it." However, once the job is done, it's done for good. Then the people can go on to learn another setting.

All this probably will call for a substantial increase in the music budget. Above everything else, the parish should employ a musician who knows his business—preferably a full-time man. Also, it will cost something to buy printed music and to mimeograph what can be so reproduced without infringement of copyright. Phonograph records and tape recordings may be helpful. Professional instrumentalists will have to be paid. A parish which desires renewal in worship should not be stingy with its allotments for music.

Small Groups

However, when everything possible has been done to arrange for a steady diet of joyful "now" services, nothing whatever has happened to foster interpersonal relationships. The lonely stranger, stimulated as he may have been by the folk music and the related spirit of good fellowship, will still be unacquainted with his fellow-worshipers, and will go home wishing that the happy communion might somehow include the formation of friendships. Somehow the family spirit ought to be developed, and on a deeper level than the usual vacuous pleasantries which are exchanged by mere acquaintances. This is manifestly impossible during a Sunday morning church service. If Christians are to discover one another and to participate in Christian community on a deep level, it will have to be in groups that are much smaller than most urban congregations. This is perhaps the basic cause of the formation of those small groups known as the underground church. The small group movement is a growing phenomenon. The purposes are various: study, prayer, self-knowledge, fellowship with others, practicing psychological techniques, and others. In all cases the program has been very serious; frivolity, for the most part, is eschewed by modern church members. This means that those who participate are determined to find some values which they have not been able to come upon in the larger congregation; and when people are so determined, they usually find what they seek. Indeed, in many instances this activity has been so rewarding that the group members tend to think of the group as their church, their congregation, particularly if a priest or minister joins with them frequently for the celebration of Holy Communion. Increasing numbers of the baptized are discovering in these more limited associations a warmth, a fellowship of faith and love which gives them more joy and peace than they had ever found in a large church on a Sunday morning.

Is this then the pattern of the future? Are we to anticipate the death of the parish and the emergence of thousands upon thousands of house churches? There are signs which make this possibility something less than fantastic. One is the success of the groups presently in existence. Another is the strong aversion of young people to construction of new church buildings, the emphasis being on human rather than material values. A third is the fact that in some services today the organ is silent, having been replaced by guitars and similar instruments which do not require the extended training and skill that are demanded of an organist. Similarly, many church choirs have ceased to function, since some expertness is required of them also. The contemporary emphasis is on simplicity and informality; it is also on the self-realization of the individual as he explores and discovers the fellowship of the Holy Spirit. This seems to happen best in small groups; there the individual finds himself, other people, and

God. At least this is what is supposed to take place; and many reports indicate that it often does.

Small Groups and Parish Structures

It is, however, very difficult to conceive of an America in which there would be no churches—or very few of them. For, whether we like it or not, some degree of organization is necessary if the church is to carry on its work. Even the primitive church had it. The apostles were the first officers; then came the deacons, with their special assignment. Soon there were prophets, teachers, readers, door-keepers, and others with specialized tasks. There was even a special offering for the relief of the saints in Jerusalem. It is not the purpose of this book to make a brief for the church as an organization, however; on the contrary, we strongly suspect that the modern church is over-organized. But if it should be that our church buildings would be closed, some precious values would be lost—perhaps irretrievably.

We have been thinking of the kind of spiritual experience in a parish that is large enough to make an extensive musical program possible. In small groups too there will be some singing, but by the very nature of the group it is bound to be strictly limited. Without the leadership of a qualified musician it may very well bog down into nothing at all.

The same rule obtains in respect to the preaching of the Word. In a situation in which there are no more parishes or church buildings there will no longer be proclamation and instruction by people who have been specially trained to give it. Clergymen, qualified as they are now by college and seminary preparation, will be nowhere nearly numerous enough to give adequate attention to the hundreds of small groups which may look to them for pastoral care. The groups will be thrown on their own resources, which to a point may be a good thing. It will force the members to do some biblical digging of their own; but there comes a point in this process beyond which it is very helpful to have professional guidance. The level of knowledge, faith, and life in the church is not likely to rise above that of its clergy. We have succeeded in developing a well-educated clergy, whatever defects may be theirs. If the parish system were to perish, this would inevitably result in marked lowering of clerical standards. We should then have a tent-making ministry, but without the theological background which was the undoubted asset of the original tentmaker who wrote much of the New Testament.

In all likelihood neither the small groups nor the parishes are going to disappear. It would be most regrettable if this happened. For both have a place in the ongoing life of the church. To say that either one is essential would be overstating the case, for the church can exist in the most exceptional circumstances; all that is really necessary is two or more people who believe the gospel. We are, however, not operating under persecution, but in a land in which religious freedom is guaranteed. We are privileged to shape our ecclesiastical structures in any way that seems best, but this does not mean that we must make a choice between the parochial system and unstructured cells. There is no reason why we can't have both, and there are compelling reasons why we need both.

We have already touched on the advantages of a large parish for the worship experience of the faithful and have suggested that the possibilities of this deserve to be further explored. What is to be said in favor of the small groups? Handled wisely, these groups may not only precipitate the enrichment of spiritual experiences for those who belong to them, but may also make an invaluable contribution to the life of the congregation. If all goes well, the group members will not regard their group activity as the end-all of their spiritual life, but, on the contrary, their Christian sensibilities will be sharpened toward other brothers and sisters in the family of God. For this is the chief virtue of small groups: to deepen people's consciousness of the communion of saints. It would be strange indeed if those who have experienced what this means in the small group interchange did not transpose what they have learned onto the larger scene. They have begun to look at other people and at themselves in a new light, and in that light they go to church on Sunday. They know that among the people of the congregation, however unacquainted they may be with one another, there lies a deep community, that its potentialities are quite wonderful, and that all of it has its source and center in the Spirit who brought them together in the first place. So they participate in congregational worship with a heightened love, joy, and peace—carry-overs from the small group experience.

Values are transposed in the opposite direction, too. This is seen most markedly in people's attitude toward the Eucharist. To a small group on a one-day weekend retreat it seems the most natural thing in the world to bring their experience to climactic expression with an informal celebration of Holy Communion. Simple vessels are used, and ordinary bread, and wine poured out of a bottle. The members of the group participate verbally in meditation on the Word, and likewise in intercessory prayer. The greeting of peace is a demonstration of warm affection. Then the consecrated elements are passed from hand to hand in an atmosphere of solemn joy and quiet peace. With the final blessing the retreat comes to an end. Often some tears are shed. The communion of saints has become very real and surprisingly wonderful.

Now consider how participation in congregational worship has paved the way for this experience. Above all else, the overriding concept of the sacrament as a meal has caught hold, so that eating and drinking in a small room, as a family, does not seem at all strange. Various practices have come to be accepted: laymen reading the lessons and suggesting intercessions, the use of "real" bread, the greeting of peace. Little by little the idea has gained ground that worship is a corporate act, in which other people beside the pastor have parts to play; it is a family meal in which the brothers and sisters rejoice in one another's company, with mother church, the Father in heaven, and their big brother. Everything is done in the Spirit, who somehow ceases to be a mere theological concept and becomes indeed the giver of life. The small group experience would be very meagre, perhaps even non-existent, if its members had not learned in church how to think of themselves, of their fellows, of God, and of the sacrament. What they do in the small group is to put this knowledge to work.

Think of it in another way: the two great commandments are to love God and love our neighbor. In congregational worship the emphasis is on the former, in group dynamics on the latter. But in neither case is the emphasis exclusive. There are some parts of the liturgy which have to do with interpersonal relationships (intercessory prayer, for example), and the preachers sometimes speak about this at length. Conversely, people who have participated in a successful retreat go home knowing that they have come closer to the Lord. The chief thrust of the one is vertical and of the other, horizontal. Thus they complement each other. There would be something seriously missing from the life of the church if the saints came together only for Sunday morning worship. On the other hand, if there were only small groups, there would be no opportunity to cultivate the art of public worship and so to sense the transcendence of God. A parish which pays close attention to both activities is making an effort to cultivate obedience to the two great commandments of the law.

In all that has been said there has been no mention of pastoral counseling or private confession and absolution. This omission should not be taken to mean a deprecation of these elements of church life. Rather, these one-to-one conversations are stimulated by the congregational and group activities we have been talking about. This is particularly true of small groups, for the pastor, to the limit of his available time, will himself be a member of the groups, and, to the extent that he participates as one of the group, will reveal himself to the others as they do to him. A valuable result of this is that his people will come to know him and to love him as a human being, and—what is very important—one whom they can trust as counselor and confessor. They will feel free to come to him as a man who will have some understanding and sympathy, as well as to a representative of the Lord, entrusted with the exercise of the Office of the Keys.

The essential business of the church, when all is said and done, is the handling of the Word and Sacraments. If some congregations are dying on the vine, it may be that they have not been "doing their thing," but have dissipated their energy in peripheral matters. If, on the other hand, there are other parishes experiencing a new surge of life, they are in all likelihood discovering new ways of using the means of grace. Surely Sunday morning is not the only time to do this. Sunday mornings and the time in between must somehow be fused into a unified, God-glorifying Christian life.

6

REVISING THE CHURCH YEAR

The most effective teaching device in the arsenal of the church has probably been the church year. By this means for many centuries Christians have annually been recalled to the great events which constitute the foundation of their faith: the birth, ministry, death, resurrection, and ascension of Jesus Christ, the coming of the Holy Spirit, and the promise of the second advent. More than this: the faithful are actually to participate in the events brought into prominence by the various seasons, so that during Advent they receive the coming Christ, at Christmas they are born anew, in the Epiphany season they behold the unfolding revelation of the Son of God, during Lent they struggle against temptation, learn to crucify the flesh, and better to appreciate the sacrifice of the Savior; in Eastertide to come out into newness of life, on Ascension Day to ascend with Christ "in heart and mind," and on Pentecost to receive a renewed portion of the Holy Spirit. Without the device of the church year it is quite possible that the church might have strayed from its moorings even more than, at certain periods, it has done. In the same way that the Book of Common Prayer has kept the Church of England on the doctrinal rails, the church year has done this for the universal church.

Church Year Problems

The story of the development of the church year is a curious one. It is not germane to our purpose to trace it here, but two things about it may help us when we undertake a revision. The first is that it is to some extent at least geared to nature. Our Lord's birth is celebrated just a few days after the winter solstice, that is, just when the sun begins to bring back its light and warmth. (We speak, of course, as inhabitants of the Northern Hemisphere, in which the scheme of the church year was developed.) The Lenten season is, weather-wise, the most disagreeable time of year, and Easter, if it is not too early, should be a day on which there is some promise of returning life to plants, grass, and trees.

The other noteworthy feature of the church year is that some of its days are related to customs and practices which are no longer in usage. The Gospels for the first three Sundays in Lent are an example. They were originally chosen to correspond with the acts of exorcism to which the catechumens, or new converts, were subjected on these days in the early church. Since that sort of catechumenate and the accompanying exorcisms are no longer in vogue in the church, these Gospels, which have to do with the devil, are anachronisms. There are other archaic tidbits to be discovered in the propers.

This is not of major importance, but it does illustrate the thesis that the traditional church year requires up-dating. Some parts of it, of course, no one would wish to change: the three great festivals, Christmas, Easter, and Pentecost, will certainly still be in the Christian calendar when the Lord comes to judgment—except that, as now seems likely, we shall have a fixed date for Easter. Aside from these high days there is not much that is truly functional. The Advent section is perhaps the best, but immediately after Christmas there is great confusion—we read about the slaughter of the children on Holy Innocents' Day, December 28, and then on Sunday after Christmas (which normally comes later) we hear about an incident connected with the Presentation of our Lord, which, however, is not officially commemorated until February 2. On top of this, we have to back up still further in time to listen to the one-verse Gospel of the Circumcision on the Octave of Christmas, and then shift mental gears once more on the Sunday following to hear the story of the flight into Egypt. It would help, of course, if we always celebrated our Savior's birth on the same day of the week, but even as things are, we should be able to arrange the Gospels a little better than that.

If and when Easter falls on the same Sunday every year, it will be possible to do something about the Epiphany season. First of all, the record of our Lord's baptism should be read somewhere along the line, perhaps the First Sunday after Epiphany. This is an important day in the calendar of the Eastern church and deserves a prominent place in our own. The Gospel of the twelve-year-old Christ in the temple would then be read on the Second Sunday, and the record of the first miracle on the Third. At this point we shall have to make up our minds whether we wish to follow the lead of the Roman Catholic church, which has been approved by the Episcopal church, in scuttling the "gesima" Sundays so that the Epiphany season would continue right up to the beginning of Lent. If so, the Gospels for the additional Epiphany Sundays would be other stories of the manifestation of Christ's glory. The Festival of the Transfiguration, which the editor of the *Service Book and Hymnal* unwisely transferred to August 6, would complete the Epiphany cycle, which then would be more ample and a better constructed season than what we have now.

We will also have to make up our minds about Lent. Should we restrict the term to denote only the time from Ash Wednesday to Judica? Shall we then in the ensuing two weeks (Passiontide) concentrate on the Savior's suffering and death, and choose some other theme for the first four weeks? If so, what shall that theme be? If it is to be the struggle between good and evil, perhaps the Gospels for the first three Sundays could be permitted to stand. The alternative would be to think of the entire 40 days as a meditation on the Passion of Christ, as Lutherans have been accustomed to do in their mid-week services. If this plan is to be followed, the Gospels for the first three Sundays ought to be more in character with this theme. (The argument that the Lenten Sundays are in Lent but not of Lent is not very convincing.) The Gospel for Laetare is such a precious thing that one would hesitate to part from it; but if one is to be rigorously consistent, one would be compelled to do so. If the question about the character of Lent were put to a vote, many ballots would be cast with a feeling that Lent as we have had it is too long for modern man, and that we would do well to return to the practice of observing a two-week period of concentration on the story of the last 40 hours of our Lord's life. What to do with the first four weeks would be an unanswered question.

No serious criticism may be made about the Gospels for Eastertide, but the season after Pentecost is something else again. The Sunday following the Pentecost is completely ambiguous: the Gospel prescribed in *The Lutheran Hymnal* is a relic of the time when the day was the Octave of Pentecost, but the rest of the propers are specifically for the Festival of the Holy Trinity. This has happily been corrected in the *Service Book and Hymnal.*

Then come the Sundays after Trinity, or, as they are designated in the Roman Catholic church and alternately in the *Service Book and Hymnal* (although not in the *Book of Common Prayer),* Sundays after Pentecost. If and when the date of Easter is fixed, there will invariably be twenty-four Sundays after Trinity, or twenty-five after Pentecost. In any event, this is a very long season, and as it is now constituted, there seems to be very little order in it; it's just one Sunday after the next, without any detectable thought progression, except at the very end, when the lessons are concerned with the last judgment.

Various attempts have been made to discover inner cycles within the season, and perhaps these inner cycles might be more sharply defined and better organized. Strodach speaks of four of these: from Pentecost to St. Peter and Paul's Day, June 29, then to St. Laurentius' Day, August 10; then to St. Michael's Day, September 29; then to Advent. It would seem that each of these cycles—or other cycles, as the church may determine—should be organized around some central theme, and that there should be orderly development from one Sunday to the next and from one cycle to the other. The nature of these themes is wide open for discussion. Dr. A. R. Kretzmann believes that there should be a succession of Sundays in the church year devoted to the doctrine of creation, and there is merit in the suggestion. Another suggestion is that there be a series of Sundays devoted to the doctrine of the church, probably immediately after Pentecost, and perhaps including as Epistles some of the marvelous sections of the Book of Acts.

If such suggestions seem too radical, consider that in any event the lectionary for the "green" half of the church year is in need of some overhauling. This brings up the whole problem of interdenominational consultation, for it would appear to be desirable that all churches which observe the ecclesiastical year do so in the same way. At present this is true only through the Third Sunday after Trinity. On the Fourth Sunday the Lutheran and Anglican Gospel is different from the Roman Catholics', and from the Fifth through the Twenty-fourth Sundays it is always one Sunday behind theirs. The Epistles are the same in all three churches, but the Anglican collects, beginning with the Fourth Sunday, are one Sunday behind the Lutheran. Obviously there has been some slipping of gears somewhere along the line, and the least that a team of interdenominational revisers should do is to get things into line again.

This would be only a superficial job, however. What needs to be done with the Trinity season is to start almost *de novo*. Some starry-eyed individuals seem to think that the church year was constructed centuries ago by some liturgical geniuses, who, because they lived in the ages of faith, selected the various propers with consummate skill and wisdom. This is clearly romantic nonsense, as may be demonstrated from a column of Epistle references of the Trinity season. The principle followed in selection was *lectio continua,* since, beginning with the Sixth Sunday after Trinity and continuing at least through the Twenty-third, most of the Pauline epistles are used in order, from Romans to Philippians—on the Twenty-sixth and the Last Sunday there are lessons from Colossians, and on the Twenty-seventh Sunday there is one from 1 Thessalonians.

In the same way, if the psalms of the offertories and the psalms of the Communions are arranged in columns, they will in every case be in numerical order. It appears that the only proper elements for these Sundays which show any possibility of careful selection are the Gospels, and no one knows what the principle of that selection may have been, except for somewhat arbitrary and haphazard items like the Gospel for the Fifth Sunday, the miraculous drought of fishes, which was chosen because the Sunday usually came near St. Peter's Day, June 29. In short, nothing hangs together; the propers have no relationship to one another, except accidentally. If we are going to be antiquarians, we will have to adhere to this mish-mash; but if we are to be intelligent, responsible churchmen, we shall do some thorough overhauling.

It would be well, at this point, to take note of the Roman Catholic scheme of a three-year cycle of lessons, a scheme which, with only minor variations, has been adopted by the Protestant Episcopal church. Lutherans must now weigh the merits and disadvatanges of such a lectionary. The idea, of course, is not new in the Lutheran church: the Church of Sweden has had a three-year lectionary, and it was suggested as an alternate in the old American Lutheran Church. To adopt such a plan would mean that particular lessons would no longer be associated in our minds with particular Sundays. On the other hand, a wider range of Scriptures would be heard in the churches, and that in itself would be a good thing. New lessons, Epistles and Gospels would be included.

Weekday Services

One of the assumptions behind the Roman Catholic lectionary is that most of the faithful are going to come to church only on Sundays. The Sunday lectionary, therefore, is independent of that prescribed for week-days. For Lutherans this is no problem; we count ourselves fortunate if our people come every Sunday! The building of the interstate highway system has aggravated the absentee situation, and the establishment, in 1971, of four long weekends per year (Washington's Birthday, Memorial Day, Columbus Day and Veterans' Day) will make it still worse. It's difficult to keep a congregation together if its members are constantly out of the city from Friday afternoon to Sunday night. Furthermore, some of the members who do stay in town must work on Sunday; in some areas stores of all kinds are open on what formerly was known as the Lord's Day. Sunday as an institution, as a day of rest and of church-going, is fast disappearing in our country. Sunday evening services, except in the south and among smaller churches, were surrendered some time ago; now it seems that Sunday morning is no longer what it was.

To bewail this development is useless; the church will simply have to find new avenues for its ministry. Perhaps a comeback of the mid-week evening service is to be anticipated. If that is to come to pass, two obstacles will have to be overcome. One of them is television—indeed a formidable attention-getter. If the church is to be more magnetic, it will have to pay careful attention to its mid-week evening services. The music, the preaching, the celebration of the sacrament will have to seem so attractive that TV will be put down as second-best. How to do this is of course a very demanding challenge. One might be averse to "gimmicks," but perhaps in an age like ours they are almost mandatory. Multi-media, dialog sermons, open-ended dramatic presentations, interpretive dancing, visiting choirs, provocative speakers—these are some of the "drawing cards" that suggest themselves to pastoral program planners. It would be much easier simply to choose three hymns and jot down a few sermon notes on a 3x5 card. If people did not turn out for that kind of service, one could complain about their despising the means of grace. But it may be that the means of grace need a new suit of clothes. Perhaps if they were dressed up in something "sharp," people would give them a second look.

TV is one obstacle to week-day services. Another is the deeply ingrained attitude, "Sunday morning or nothing." How this attitude developed is quite understandable. It's a carry-over from an earlier age in which everybody in Christian communities and families went to Sunday services as a matter of course. Then the changes came, with mounting acceleration: the automobile, chiefly; 'round the clock factory work during the war; television most of all.

In former times, Lutheran churches had no mid-week services; they were not necessary. What is now necessary, apparently, is an intensive attitude-changing campaign which would emphasize the importance of once-a-week participation in corporate worship, whether on Sunday or some other day. The church, engaged as it is in a struggle for its own survival, needs to hammer away on the idea that once-a-week church attendance is a self-imposed obligation of a Christian, and that if circumstances make it impossible to fulfill this obligation on one day, he is to do it on another. Perhaps in some areas churches might agree to hold services at different times through the week, so that no one could claim that the week-day hour did not suit him any better than Sunday morning. Robbing people of excuses for non-attendance is one way of separating the men from the boys. A sifting process is at work in our time, and if there are people on our parish rosters who really don't care whether the church lives or dies, we'd better find it out and purge their names from our files.

Week-day services all through the year would have some effect on the seasonal week-day services which have been traditionally held in Lutheran churches. Mid-week Lenten services are the out-

97

standing example. What is to become of these? Attendance at Lenten services has been declining. People just don't like Lent anymore—if they ever did. It's too long a season, for one thing. For another, it is too severe for our easygoing, affluent, pleasure-loving society. Talk about fasting, struggle against sin, and repentance turns people off. Preaching about the crucifixion strikes them as morbid, oppressive, ugly. They don't want to hear it. They don't want to go to church anyhow. They have been working all day, they are tired, and there is a special on TV that they want to see. Why subject themselves to gloomy thoughts about suffering and death when they can relax in front of the "boob tube"? The observance of Lent is not what it used to be.

The same is true, only more so, of Ascension Day, Reformation Day, All Saints' Day, St. Michael's Day, and many other minor festivals which once may have been generally observed in the church. Our generation doesn't even know what day it is and couldn't care less. The suggestion has therefore been made that the church give up trying to observe these festivals on the designated day and transfer them to the nearest Sunday. This, however, interrupts any progression of thought which might be detected in the revised Sunday propers, virtually eliminating certain Sundays from the church year, since the festivals would annually occur in roughly the same week. This would be unfortunate.

If, however, we can propagandize the notion that corporate worship is just as much in order on week-days as it is on Sundays and consequently build up attendance at the mid-week service, these festivals can be transposed to the day on which the services are customarily held. In such cases the ordinary service will become extraordinary, so that the festival will be a real celebration, conducted in an atmosphere of infectious joy. It will take time for a practice like this to become popular, but with careful nurturing the job can be done. Maybe even Lent can be rescued from oblivion.

Perhaps too this may lead to the refurbishing of the sanctoral cycle. The minor holy days presently on our calendar will stand a much better chance of being observed if they can be transferred to the day on which the mid-week service is held. Particularly in these instances there will be a celebration of Holy Communion, for these days have their own propers. This, however, does not exclude the possibility of other days being added to the calendar.

As it now stands, only New Testament saints are commemorated in Lutheran churches. But there is no good reason why other men and women from various centuries, including our own, should not be so remembered, for sanctity and distinguished service to Christ did not cease with the death of the last apostle. The problem is setting up criteria to make a judicious selection of outstanding saints. Whose names shall appear on the list? Who shall be excluded? On what basis? The difficulty of making choices is not so great as to cause us to give the whole thing up. Lutherans should be aware of the existence of the church of Christ both before and after the Reformation. This would help cultivate a catholic consciousness; it would enlarge our concept of the church.

Taking the Secular into Account

Let us return to our consideration of the Sunday cycle. It is true of course that the church year has a genius all its own which should not be disturbed by all sorts of secular intrusions. Most pastors have the good sense to deposit the frequent appeals for special Sundays (with special offering, of course) into the round file on the floor by the side of the desk. Churches can easily be derailed from their chief task by dissipating their interest and energy in these endless extraneous projects.

Nevertheless, in the refashioning of the church year perhaps some attention should be paid to the secular pulse. Thus, if preparations for Christmas begin on the Thanksgiving Day weekend, as in fact they do, then it would seem logical that the Advent season should begin on that Sunday, rather than on the Sunday nearest St. Andrew's Day, as the rubric presently prescribes. And if the ensuing weeks, in the lives of most Christian people, are a time of mounting expectancy of Christmas, why shouldn't the propers of the season reflect this, rather than confuse the faithful with Gospels about the Palm Sunday entrance and the second coming of Christ? Let thoughts about the parousia be reserved for some other time; in Advent we light our candles in anticipation of the Feast of the Nativity. And this doesn't seem to be an appropriate season for penitence, either!

Shall we pay some ecclesiastical attention to the long weekends? Pentecost will often take precedence over Memorial Day, and Thanksgiving Day has some religious connotations of its own, but there would be no great harm in recognizing the significance of Independence Day and Labor Day. Possibly, if we are to think in terms of cycles during the long Pentecost season, we might designate these two days as dividing points, so that the first cycle (which might be concerned with the establishment of the church as described in the Acts of the Apostles) would run from Pentecost to Independence Day; the second cycle (which might have to do with the works of God in nature and in the contemporary world) would extend to Labor Day; and the last cycle (which might be centered in eschatology) to the end of the church year. Independence Day and Labor Day would not be part of any of the cycles, but would stand on their own merits.

It would be refreshing to have a different emphasis in the spring of the year. If Lent is losing its traditional place in the experience of the faithful, let there be a new focusing on the joy of Eastertide. Easter is different from Christmas. There's a lot of building up to Christmas, so that on the day after the feast everyone is exhausted, but there is no building up to Easter; it bursts in on the church, almost unexpectedly. Lent is no preparation for it; Lent has values of its own. Therefore the message of the resurrection ought not be confined to one day; it deserves to be the theme of the entire 50 days. Some of the propers do this—certainly those for Quasimodogeniti. But the church ought to take a new look at the whole season. We're definitely in favor of upgrading Eastertide.

Lutherans are beginning the task of reforming the church year and the lectionary rather late in the day. The Roman Catholics and the Episcopalians have already finished their work and are starting to implement the changes. The ILCW hopefully will conform as closely as possible to their findings. Some variations there are bound to be, but these should be minor ones, so that the great liturgical churches will have the same annual rhythm as they seek to review and relive the events of redemption and as they undertake to make pertinent applications of the gospel to the world in which they live.

7

A WORD ON SPONTANEITY

In the foregoing chapters the discussion has centered around various aspects of liturgical reform: the structure of the Eucharist, the up-dating of language, the musical settings of the Eucharist, ceremonies, the church year. Revisions in all these areas have been approved by various liturgical commissions—and the end is not yet in sight.

Now the cry is heard in the land that these changes are not radical enough, that what is needed is spontaneity. Proponents of spontaneity are not entirely clear on what they mean by the word. If they wish merely to allow an occasional "Amen" from some emotionally stirred worshiper, or an "Hallelujah" or "Praise the Lord," perhaps liturgical commissioners might raise no strenuous objection, although they might raise an eyebrow slightly. If, however, spontaneity means that nothing is to be planned in advance, that the entire service is to be impromptu, the same commissioners would probably disapprove—perhaps quite strenuously.

For one thing, spontaneity of this sort is obviously incompatible with liturgy. If the faithful are to rely on the impulse of the moment, they cannot refer to a printed form. Maybe this would be just as well—but only if those concerned were well versed in the Word of God, had a good understanding of the essential elements of corporate worship and the sequence of these elements best suited to the psychology of men, and lastly and most importantly, were filled with the Holy Spirit. The bishops of the early church were sometimes permitted to pray according to their ability; there is a rubric to that effect, for instance, in the liturgy of Hippolytus. But it was always assumed that these men were deeply spiritual and that they knew what needed to be included in a eucharistic prayer. Never in any ancient liturgy—and in very few modern ones—is any provision made for laymen popping up all over the church with various ejaculations or even *ex corde* prayers. This is not said to oppose the contemporary practice of permitting people to call out, at the time of the great intercession, "Let us pray for. . . ." That is spontaneity within structure, and there is little criticism of this. What is down-right appalling to lovers of liturgy is the proposal that there is to be no preliminary planning, except for a general and vague idea of the objectives to be sought and the methods to be used for their attainment.

There will inevitably be more spontaneity in small group worship than in a large congregation, more in an outdoor setting at a summer camp than in a great cathedral, more in a less cultured group than in a highly sophisticated gathering. Yet in every case certain basic principles obtain, which may be listed as follows:

1. The worship of God is too serious a project to be undertaken thoughtlessly. If sometimes quite elaborate preparations are made to meet a distinguished human being, how much more attention ought to be paid to our corporate encounters with God in Christ! Like marriage, it ought not to be entered into "unadvisedly or lightly, but reverently, discretely, and in the fear of God."

2. The God we worship is a God of order, not chaos. And reports about certain liturgical happenings have indicated that these have been rather chaotic. Creation requires not merely the word, but, presumably, the thought which antedates the word. There is some mind behind the action, and some plan which comes forth from the mind. God does not do things with no idea of what is going to happen next. Neither should his disciples.

3. Human beings cannot react without having something to which it is possible to react. They cannot be expected to come together and begin

jumping for joy for no discernible reason. There must be some provocation, some word, some portrayal, some music to stir the soul. It helps a great deal if this initial incitement is planned in advance.

4. Complete spontaneity carries with it the possibilities of emotional excess and theological shallowness. The cry today is: Celebrate. And everyone is in favor of celebrating. Why not? But what is it which the Christian community is to celebrate? This should be well defined, lest the church settle for some species of naturalism which falls far short of an acknowledgment of the Lord Jesus Christ. It is good to be joyful in God's creation; it is better to be thankful for redemption.

5. Human psychology must be taken into consideration. This means that a liturgy should be geared to the principle that a spiritual adventure usually begins with a state of inertia, then is sparked by some eternal influence, and finally "rises higher, takes fire" in a series of mounting climaxes. If a liturgy is to be constructed so delicately, it obviously needs to be well worked out in advance. When nobody takes the trouble to find out what makes people tick, it is not to be wondered at if they don't tick very rapidly in church.

6. Finally, it is basic to this whole problem that the subject is corporate worship, not individ-

ual expression. This means that the worshipers must agree on what they are to do before they do it. Exactly how is the agreement to be brought about? Is the group first to participate in a business meeting, with votes taken on each hymn to be sung, each prayer to be spoken? Most people would have little patience with such a procedure, and many would not feel qualified to make the judgments required of them. They would be content to leave the planning of the service to the liturgical and hymnological experts, which would include both those on the parish staff and those serving on the official committees and commissions of the church. These persons, as they themselves would cheerfully admit, are not infallible, but, by reason of their training and their awareness of the situation in the contemporary church, are much more likely to arrange a meaningful service.

The Holy Spirit definitely moves the hearts and minds of the laity, and surely no clergyman should ever be caught trying to quench this Spirit. On the other hand, if there is to be any organization in the church, any assignment of tasks, surely the most obvious people to handle matters of worship are the pastors and the musicians. If they are wise, they will not choose music and forms which are beyond the capabilities of the people they serve. They will lead the congregation one step at a time into the unknown land of the experience of worship. This can be a thrilling adventure, and it will be that if competence is permitted to override both arrogant destruction of what is old, and fumbling inexpert attempts to produce the new.

The eighth decade of the 70s will hopefully see some of the dust settle. It's been a hectic century up to now, and probably its pace will not slacken in the time to come. But liturgical innovation has its limits. One may revise the inheritance, modernize it, supply it with strange music; it will still retain its basic outline, and for some time to come, its inherited imagery. What is more, most congregations will not tolerate too much change at one time. Parishioners must be given time to assimilate one ceremony or setting of the liturgy before passing on to something else. To introduce these things skillfully, with a minimum of negative reaction, requires considerable insight and skill of the pastor, who, among much else, has been trained to teach people to worship. Let him fulfill his function then. And let him make ample use of the experience of the ages and the productions of liturgical commissions. Perhaps in this way we can have peace with progress and a richer worship experience than we have ever known.